4.28.09

GARDEN
Whimsy

GARDEN
Whimsy

Text by Tovah Martin

Photographs by
Richard W. Brown

A Frances Tenenbaum Book

Houghton Mifflin Company
Boston New York 1999

For information about permission to reproduce selections from this book,
write to Permissions, Houghton Mifflin Company, 215 Park Avenue South,
New York, New York 10003.

Library of Congress Cataloging-in-Publication Data

Martin, Tovah

Garden whimsy / text by Tovah Martin ;
photographs by Richard W. Brown.

p.   cm.

"A Frances Tenenbaum book."

ISBN 0-395-93731-0

1. Gardening   I. Title.

SB455.M3689   1999

635.9—dc21

Frontispiece: GLOVED FENCE, MOIR GARDEN, LYME, NEW HAMPSHIRE

Book design by Susan McClellan

Printed in the United States of America

DOW 10 9 8 7 6 5 4 3 2 1

BOOKS BY TOVAH MARTIN AND RICHARD W. BROWN

Tasha Tudor's Garden
Tasha Tudor's Heirloom Crafts
Garden Whimsy

READING FROG,
LES QUATRE VENTS,
LA MALBAIE, QUEBEC

Contents

Introduction

HEARD AN UNUSUAL SOUND IN A GARDEN THE OTHER DAY. It wasn't the song of a migratory bird, it wasn't the tinkle of wind chimes or the gurgle of a fountain. Instead, I caught the music of a delighted laugh floating from the shrubbery. I peered around the corner and saw the source of the merriment: it was a little plaque, stuck in the bed, that read GROW, DAMN IT. I saw it as a good sign.

Heaven knows we could use a little levity in the garden. Knee deep in compost, preoccupied with axial symmetry, and engrossed by integrated pest management, gardeners suffer from a tendency to take themselves too seriously. Granted, gardening is hard work accomplished only by considerable brow sweat and backache. There are predators to battle, weeds to expel, and branches to prune. All that serious business is exactly why a garden is the perfect place for some lightheartedness. If we must have thorns, then we might as well make a fence that pays homage to their prickliness. If there are spiders in the garden, then a gigantic spiderweb gate provides the perfect exclamation point.

*T*HERE'S NOTHING new about horticultural humor, of course. Whimsy crept into the landscape long ago. When you think about it, there's something inherently absurd about taking a plot of land and cramming the place with blossoms, spiraling shrubs, squarely snipped hedges, or what have you. And so, building on that foundation of disbelief, all gardens are a little askew. Filled with flowers from five continents growing unnaturally side by side, sporting fountains in the desert, or marching bravely up breakneck hillsides, all gardens are a suspension of reality.

But some are a little more offbeat than others. The British in particular have a tradition of incorporating whimsy into their grounds. In the eighteenth century they began littering their landscapes with follies, false ruins, temples dedicated to all sorts of mythical creatures, topiary peacocks and chess pieces. Technology just made matters worse. By the nineteenth century there were trick water jets that gushed up ladies' crinolines or squirted into gentlemen's eyes when they trod on a certain paving stone, and mirrors that fooled weary pedestrians into fearing that a path continued indefinitely. Gargoyles, sea serpents, scantily clad maidens, naked nymphs, mermaids, and whatever ancient god or goddess you wished to have at your beck and call were represented in statuary form. Egyptian tombs and tunnels with trick passageways sprang up. Legend has it that one inventive lord devised a garden of special narrow allées that his slender mistress could slip through — but not his hefty wife. The British might maintain a stiff upper lip, but they are also fond of their puns. And let us never forget that Britain was the birthplace of the pointy-capped, potbellied garden gnome. Tongue-in-cheek is certainly not virgin turf.

Somehow all the merriment didn't translate over here at first. It takes a measure of confidence to throw caution to the wind, and originally we

Americans were much too busy beating back the wilderness to find appetite for cheerful abandon. Tidy little symmetrical herb gardens were all we could muster at the outset. Then, when we gained a modicum of control, we had suburbia to render homogenous — not a task to be toyed with. What followed was a time of tyranny when red geraniums reigned.

Sooner or later, though, American landscapes were bound to lighten up. At long last, snippets of whimsy are beginning to crop up everywhere. Gardeners are feeling their oats, flexing their muscles, and cracking a grin. The result is a proliferation of daringly dressed scarecrows, wacky watering devices, expressive birdhouses, and weird whirligigs. The sky's the limit.

E'RE NOT TALKING slapstick here; I don't mean wholesale silliness or the latest cute little cement bunny that you encountered at your discount garden center. No, true whimsy has its basis in creativity. It's practiced by people who see things from a slightly different angle. You find it in the back yards of gardeners who are brave and perhaps slightly irreverent as well. Nothing is sacred, there are no rules, and the practice of gardening doesn't present a problem that they can't poke fun at. Whimsical gardeners tend to be outspoken. More than proficient, they're often the experts. They're sophisticated enough to occasionally play it straight . . . or not. Sometimes they're subtle; sometimes they're brazen. But one thing is certain — they don't care what the neighbors think of their color combinations or their taste. I see them as the trendsetters. Take their precedent and run. ❧

BRONZE CROW,
LEVINE GARDEN,
KENT, CONNECTICUT

Downtown Ely Gardens:
THE *S*ISTER ACT

O GET THE PUNCHLINE OF "Downtown Ely Gardens," you've got to know something about Ely (pronounced "Ee-lee"), Vermont. The town's population is well below one hundred, probably fewer than fifty. There is no downtown. Fortunately, a friend clued me in. "If you go searching for a Main Street, you'll drive right by Ely," she warned.

Well, you probably wouldn't really drive by — because the garden is enough to stop traffic. More than once, Carol Eaton and Michelle Billings, the sisters responsible for the garden, have been disturbed from their heavy weeding by the screech of brakes and have watched a car back up so the driver can get a better look at the riot of flowers packed cheek by jowl into their small front yard. In midsummer, when

■ *Opposite:*

Downtown Ely's birdhouses are purely functional. In fact, there's competition to set up housekeeping where no commute is necessary.

■ *Left:*

The airplane made its first appearance on a Fourth of July float. "We figured that the flamingo would create instant location recognition," Michelle says.

"I don't know what it is
with me and hot pink,"
says Michelle, but she's
gone through many
cans of that hue.

■ *Right:*

"At first, nothing could
be further from us than
flamingos," says Carol.
"Now we're searching
for them." In their quest
for ornaments of every
vintage, the sisters
sometimes find versions
that no longer display
their true colors, which
Michelle refers to as
"faded flamingos."

it gets rolling, Downtown Ely Gardens spills over with delphiniums, foxgloves, coneflowers, cosmos, snapdragons, cleomes, and daisies.

"When we first arrived," Carol explains, "it was sort of dead here."

"Ely was once a hopping place, we've been told," Michelle continues. "But that was a hundred years ago."

So the sisters figured they'd remedy the situation. "The owner of the nursery where we purchased

plants always parceled out standard instructions with our purchases," recalls Carol. "He advised us to plant them in rows. Truth is, I couldn't plant in rows if my life depended on it." That might explain the floral confusion.

OF COURSE, IT'S NOT ONLY the lure of looking at flowers that inspires passersby to screech to a halt. There's also the promise of taking home a bouquet, or perhaps something more

■ *A b o v e :*

What good is a gazing ball if it doesn't convey some revelation? This one reveals the stark naked "bathing beauty."

■ *L e f t :*

Cynthia Taylor, a local artist, decided that the sisters needed a man in the garden.

■ Carol and Michelle don't waste much time hunting for their artifacts. "The stuff just comes to us," they say, speaking of the Mexican pickle jar, "and we can't part with some of it."

substantial — like a wooden airplane replica.

As is often the case with such ventures, the two sisters weren't planning to begin a thriving business when they purchased a couple of rundown bungalows and a parcel just shy of three acres on Ely's somniferous main drag in 1990. Carol was in the auction business, Michelle worked for a garden center, and both were newly divorced, so they decided to strike out on a joint venture. "As I recall," Michelle, the younger sister, reminisces, "we were just going to sell birdbaths." Looking to Carol for encouragement, she forges on. "It started with birdbaths, but then it just sort of evolved . . ."

Now Carol and Michelle sell everything from garden ornaments (funky and otherwise) to furniture painted shocking shades.

"At first we wouldn't think of selling an elf or a gnome," says Carol.

"We thought they were trashy," Michelle corroborates. "But now we love elves."

They deal in bits of architectural debris, fountains, scarecrows (either preclothed or dress-your-own), wind

chimes, gazing balls, and trellises in addition to cut flowers.

The birdbaths have segued into water gardens. The first one, in front of their shop, was strictly a makeshift affair. "We did it in a day. We went out onto the interstate and gathered some rocks. We put in a bridge, some wind chimes, things that spouted water, lots of frogs, and the water lilies, of course," Carol explains. Now, savvy about liners and building materials, they are in demand locally for their expertise and have installed a number of creative water features.

THE FLIGHTS OF concrete fancy certainly fuel some of the drive-by double takes, but the garden has plenty going for it from a horticultural standpoint as well. There too all the stops have been pulled out. Flowers flourish in a profusion that is almost frightening. And the location is perfect to support the enterprise. "The river takes care of us," says Michelle cryptically. The statement turns out to be more than rhetoric: the soil on their parcel is composed of such fertile riverbottom stuff that the sisters scarcely need to add manure. Dreamy mists rise from the river every morning, and the water moderates temperatures to make the location Zone 5, a claim that few other places in Vermont's Northeast Kingdom can substantiate. The spot doesn't have blackflies or mosquitoes to speak of. Even the deer are dissuaded by the water barrier. In a nutshell, the garden is an enchanted place. "Everything just wants to grow," says Carol.

People mingle with the flowers and the atmosphere and add their own little spin. One magical time, a customer returned with designs for a labyrinth to be incorporated into the meadow. On other occasions, stranger things have happened. "Once someone left a message on the answering machine to say that she'd just dropped off a fairy for our garden," Carol recalls. When I look at her in disbelief, Michelle joins in, adding, "Oh yes, she gave us a complete description of the fairy and what she was wearing when last seen." The sisters both roll their eyes as they tell the tale, but I think they sort of enjoy the idea.

■ The pedestal is faux cement, and none too stable, "but it holds together," Michelle says, "and who can complain for five bucks?" That's what they paid at a yard sale. It supports a portulaca — in hot pink, of course.

*A*S ANYONE WHO has ever ventured into horticulture is aware, it is dominated by a faction that is easily obsessed. Whatever the flavor of the season happens to be — blood-red-leaved penstemon with white flowers, variegated hostas, or whatever — it's all the rage. Apparently such trends have penetrated as far north as Ely. "We have a lot of friends who are plant nuts," Carol divulges.

Sure enough, when heracleum, otherwise known as giant hogweed, hit vogue, the sisters felt they had to incorporate it into their garden — only to discover that it causes a severe skin rash that rivals the one caused by poison ivy. Not only that, the plant is invasive. And it stands taller than six feet.

"I fear," Carol says, thinking about the situation, "that we've created a monster."

Michelle is equally concerned. "We'll be out there with machetes," she agrees.

Carol, warming to the idea, adds, "We'll be out there with chainsaws and full body suits."

With that image, the owners of Downtown Ely Gardens, specializing in larkspur and lingerie, burst into torrents of laughter. 🙙

■ "The petunias and phlox were purely accidental," insists Michelle. "In fact, the phlox came from an old farm north of here." The 'Heavenly Blue' morning glories were intentional.

BEAUTIES AND THE BEASTS

LIKE OVERALLS TRANSMOGRIFIED INTO DESIGNER jeans, some other formerly essential and practical garden elements have been usurped for a more glittering lifestyle. Scarecrows are a case in point. In the past, if you had a field of newly planted corn, you had to devise some method of deterring crows. From a purely economic standpoint, scarecrows were definitely cheap labor. (Whether they worked or not is another matter entirely.)

Initially, there was nothing ornamental about a scarecrow. Stuffed with hay, clad in your cast-off rags, a real scarecrow wouldn't be caught dead in the perennial borders of the Upper Crust. Anyway, who needed a scarecrow to protect the columbines? They were banished to backyard vegetable gardens and agricultural fields where they might best ply their trade far from human eyes.

GERTRUDE JEKYLL, STONE CROP, COLD SPRING, NEW YORK

Of course, it's different nowadays. No longer part of the working class, scarecrows frequent the best of circles, and they dress accordingly.

My family never had a scarecrow. Instead, we had my mother-in-law. Promptly at 4:30 P.M., just after

PROM QUEEN, BOND GARDEN, PEACHAM, VERMONT

BOHEMIAN SCARECROW, GEORGE GARDEN, SHELBURNE, VERMONT

taking afternoon tea and cake, my mother-in-law would march into the back yard with a skillet and spoon, bang them briskly for precisely five minutes, and then return just as determinedly indoors. It never did a bit of good as far as scaring the crows was concerned. In fact, at one time I held strongly to the theory that they convened regularly just to enjoy the concert. But it definitely kept mischievous boys and wandering dogs out of the flower beds.

II.

Lark and Rick Levine:

*S*TATUES AND LIBERTIES

VISIT THE LEVINE GARDEN in Kent, Connecticut, during one of their tour days and your first encounter is likely to be with Rick, directing traffic. "Start with the view of the stream," he'll advise, "and work your way up to the lemonade on the patio. If you have any questions, don't ask me. Ask my wife, Lark — she'll be somewhere close to the lemonade." That's not false modesty on Rick's part. A film director, Rick Levine knows everything about angles, views, and viewpoints, but his knowledge of plants is nonexistent. Which is why

■ *Opposite:*

Lark likes to think that this Joy Brown statue keeps an ear cocked for whispered confidences.

■ *Left:*

Every year Lark reshuffles the borders and displays fewer plants from the "waltz phase" in her development as a designer, in favor of more daring color combinations.

he is safely assigned to channeling the pedestrian flow around the forty-acre property. "You don't want to miss anything," he'll advise. "There's a shade garden by the stream, a vegetable bed up above, several flower borders, a grass garden around the pool, and a wildflower walk. And don't skip the little midget garden tucked on the side of the house; it's small but very effective."

So begins your trek around a curvaceous property with so many highlights that even as a casual visitor you're left breathless. The place is exhausting, which might explain why Lark stations herself centrally beside the lemonade to field inquiries. There you'll find her, energetic, outspoken, and deeply tanned, obviously the horticultural half of the team. Like any hands-on gardener, Lark spends tour days drowning her sorrows in lemonade (presumably) while apologizing for the lilies that the deer pruned or bemoaning the alpines that the chipmunks unceremoniously carried off from the stone steps. "Don't worry, Lark," says Rick, always on hand to mollify his wife when disaster occurs.

■ You've got to work as a team when you have a small herd of ostriches to entertain. Rick found the ideal spot ("complete with marooned boulder in desperate need of definition"), then Lark managed to put Peter Woytuk's bronze creations in the perfect perspective plantwise.

■ Next to the vegetable garden, as a focal point amid the adjoining formal parterre, nothing but the lipstick shades of a stellated icosahedron would do.

"We'll rip it all out tomorrow and lay gravel instead."

The garden is never good enough for Lark. In fact, yesterday's glory is a subject that so often creeps into Lark's litany that Rick finally had a disclaimer cast in bronze. MY GARDEN WAS AT ITS PEAK LAST WEEK, the plaque reads. SORRY YOU MISSED IT.

Expectations are often high with a garden started from scratch. When Rick, Lark, and their son, Stefan, arrived on the scene in 1988, they were lured by a very enticing array of buildings and outbuildings, but there was no garden to speak of. Indeed,

one scene was in desperate need of editing. The striking old mill that commands your attention when you first drive in was hardly an eyesore, but it definitely required shoring up. Next the Levines installed what Rick refers to as "the Kent subway" to provide the drainage necessary for nurturing any-thing other than water plants. Then there was the wilderness to beat back. Rather than banishing the flora, as several local arborists advised, Lark opted to selectively thin what was in place. Since everything was over-grown to a bizarre degree, she decided on parody as the best approach. It was

■ Standing eight feet tall, the Levines' "Ultimate Gazing Ball" is a force to be reckoned with.

just a hop, a skip, and a jump, for example, to trimming a grove of ancient locusts embedded in a mass of barberry into a scene that Lark calls "Balls and Sticks." The barberry is clipped into perfectly round squat orbs; the locusts — which jut straight toward heaven — are trimmed naked from the neck down.

Balls and Sticks is one of the subtler bits of sacrilege on the place. Across the stream, there's Lark's

"Dr. Seuss Garden," conceived as a vegetable plot but evolved (via Lark's convoluted mind) into a space filled with almost nothing edible. Barbed nightshades guard the gates, morning glories mount the pole to the birdhouse, and Spanish flag obliterates the fence. It's a free-for-all of twisting and climbing plants that aren't appetizing even if they're edible — like sinister midnight-podded beans, devilishly colored peppers, and guppy-shaped cucumbers with horns. Weird shapes tussle. Spiny textures brush one against the other. The assemblage is almost

an auto-body shop. In its new life as a contemporary sculpture, the "stellated icosahedron" draws your eye. Like a magnet. As Rick distills his inspiration, "When Lark does something, I heighten it."

The uncompromisingly colored star definitely captures your attention if you aren't already contemplating Rick's most recent creation, an eight-foot silver gazing ball poised precariously at the top of the hill.

never harvested for salads, but it amuses Stefan no end.

ADJACENT TO THE Dr. Seuss spectacle, the same fenced area protects a small, formal French parterre. It would be perfectly serious except for the large, shiny, cherry-red star in the center. The Levines purchased the twenty-point star, a French antique, for a song and then spent a fortune trying to weld the seams and render it weather-tolerant. Nothing worked until they took it to

■ *Overleaf:*

There's a running argument over the sex of the androgynous trio frozen in the middle of a political discussion beside the mill. Rick confesses that he has always been tempted to nestle next to one of them and "pat her on the butt," which might explain the reserved space on the bench. However, they'll always be the Pillsbury Doughboys to me.

Other pieces accent other places. A hen, with meaty body but small cranial cavity, presides over the pool garden, framed in several hundred feet of ornamental grasses, which were supposed to be low maintenance. Elsewhere there's a bronze mountain goat tottering on a precipice and a herd of life-size bronze ostriches grazing on the lawn, both by the local sculptor Peter Woytuk. They spark conversation, but the crows, also Woytuk's creation, are the favorite sculptural feature by far. Engaged in the kind of social communion that crows do so well, perched on the railing of the mill, the dozen or so birds are lifelike and ingenious. To sustain the ruse up the hill, Rick installed a lone crow on an upended slab of stone, looking as if he just left Edgar Allan Poe's chamber.

Although the sculpture evokes comment, all the while it's hedged in assiduous horticulture. The repertoire of plants is strictly that of a connoisseur. Meanwhile, borders of color wax and fade in sympathetic hues that aren't what you'd call catholic. But they work.

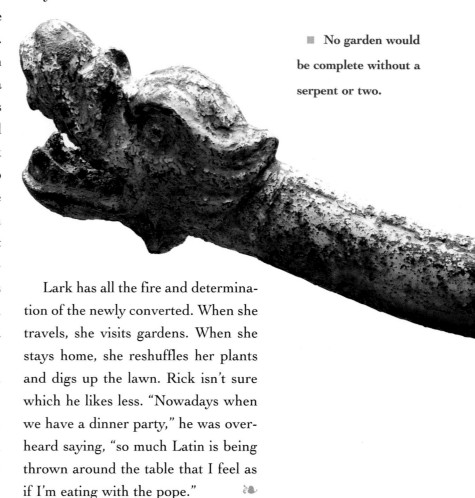

■ No garden would be complete without a serpent or two.

Lark has all the fire and determination of the newly converted. When she travels, she visits gardens. When she stays home, she reshuffles her plants and digs up the lawn. Rick isn't sure which he likes less. "Nowadays when we have a dinner party," he was overheard saying, "so much Latin is being thrown around the table that I feel as if I'm eating with the pope." ❧

PLEASE BE SEATED

I COULD NEVER UNDERSTAND GARDEN BENCHES. Although they're always placed at points that command a good view, they are rarely comfortable. Most of the time, they're downright otherwise.

For years I wondered about this. Why would anyone bother installing something that was so ill suited to its purpose? And then a friend demonstrated that benches do their appointed job perfectly. "You never sit in your garden," he pointed out. "And when visitors settle down, do you really want them to stay?"

Garden Whimsy

III.

The Sagendorf Follies:
PARTNERS IN GRIME

EVERY ONCE IN A WHILE (but not often enough), two people who were meant to be together find each other. Kit and Marty Sagendorf are a case in point. They both have an offbeat sense of humor, and they both pursue the hobby of collecting with an intemperance that might easily bury any unlike-minded partner. They come by their funny bones honestly: Kit is a cartoonist by profession; Marty is a physicist, but his father drew the comic strip *Popeye*.

Rather than competing in their urge to acquire, the Sagendorfs balance

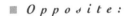

■ *Opposite:*

Everything in Home Farm had a purpose, although many of the functions have been lost. Still, Marty will make up uses for anything lacking.

■ *Left:*

It all began with a cabinet too cumbersome to fit into the Sagendorfs' stuffed-to-the-brim Victorian house. So started the building of Home Farm, a project that monopolized two solid years.

43

each other out, pile for pile. Marty goes weak-kneed when confronted with anything connected with antique electrical gadgets, old machine tools, and standard-gauge model trains, among other things. Reveal even the slightest glimmer of interest and you'll be ushered into Marty's radio room, stacked with every pre-1940 receiver and transmitter imaginable. Kit, in contrast, is powerless to resist a garden miniature or any sort of antique garden tool (especially obscure British utensils whose purpose is not readily apparent). She has also been known to take scenic detours into dollhouse furniture that has no obvious link with horticulture.

Both Sagendorfs get flushed in the face at the sight of British and American regulation croquet sets. (Don't ask them to explain the difference between the two. Kit sums it up in two words — "Americans cheat.") They also hyperventilate in near proximity to butler boxes; seven were installed in their pantry, at last count. Kit is the one who actually acquired the annunciators, as the bell systems for summoning servants are called in

■ *Opposite:*

Marty describes the architecture of Home Farm as "an amalgamation of everything." Although Marty did the primary carpentry for the project, Kit performed some finishing work. In a nutshell, she sums up the division of labor: "Marty is the finesse, I'm the unskilled labor."

■ Kit has a fetish for miniatures, especially if they can be linked (however loosely) with the outdoors. No matter that few are on the same scale: "That sort of adds to the suspension of reality."

Britain, but she claims they were installed for Marty's amusement. "He keeps ringing for the maid, but she never comes," Kit says.

AS YOU CAN imagine, not only is the house burdened by these combined predilections, but the entire property feels the brunt when flea-market season is in full swing. Because electrical equipment tends to be sensitive to weather, most of Marty's apparatus is stashed in the recesses of the couple's cavernous three-story Victorian house, which is conveniently equipped with a goodly number of spare rooms poised to receive the fallout from flea markets. But during the summer his stuff often spills onto the porch (the better to putter with, my dear), and parts from whatever 1940s tractor he happens to be restoring end up in the driveway, making for some rather dicey footing on the way to the garden. On any summer weekend afternoon you'll find Marty fiddling over a disassembled piece of equipment, pipe in mouth and oil on fingers, apologizing for having to pass up a proper handshake. He's more than willing, though, to provide a nut-by-bolt description of exactly what he's doing, in detail that would be painful except that it is always served with cold drinks in a shady spot. Nowadays the shady spot is usually at the edge of the garden and in the shadow of the property's proudest new feature — a building that the Sagendorfs refer to as Home Farm, a name they borrowed from the Agatha Christie mystery *The Body in the Library*.

Home Farm, a glorified garden shed, isn't the family's first such facility. Several years ago, Kit, who prides herself on rivaling Marty with a hammer, built a rather ornate Gothic storage shed to house her tools. It still stands, but, as is often the case with storage units, upon completion it was already overflowing. One afternoon when Kit returned from a yard sale laden with the perfect cabinet to display her collection of

■ Perhaps it was once a pint-size cold frame or a propagation box, but Kit likes to call the small glass unit her greenhouse — "probably the only one I'll ever claim."

miniatures, she realized she had no place to put it. Next thing you know, she was laying out plans for an elaborate French-doored, antique-windowed, overhung-roofed storage unit. Kit and Marty joke that they are the only gardeners in town with a focal point that took two years to make and required the continual scrutiny of the building inspector.

As fate would have it, the garden was already in a state of flux when Home Farm was under construction. "Upheaval" would be a better word. Kit began the garden in 1977, the year after they moved into the house. It was nip and tuck for the first few seasons, especially since neither of the Sagendorfs knew a jot about tilling the soil. The only certainty was that they wanted the place to feel authentic inside and out. The same forces that provoked them to hide all the house phones in closets and throw out the electric stove in favor of a wood-fueled version (which effectively ruled out any thought of baking in summer) also prevailed when they considered the adjacent plantings.

Design wasn't difficult; Victorian was the only way to go. But they lacked fundamental knowledge. Kit turned to a local garden club for advice and received the pearl of wisdom that weeds could readily be identified by their fuzzy leaves. "Safe in that understanding, I went around eradicating every Oriental poppy in sight," she says. It turned out that the poppies were the only worthwhile flowers on the property.

So the Sagendorf garden was a clean slate in 1977 when they began working on the plantings flanking several exposures of the imposing house, and the scene was rendered nearly blank again twenty years later when a freak tornado took down several trees on the property, a date Marty refers to as "the Big Bang." In addition to the splintering of urns, perennials, and fences at the trees' point of impact, there were residual effects, such as the yard's sudden transformation from a shade garden to a sunny scene.

The tornado provided a good excuse for a complete facelift. This time around, the couple tossed caution to the wind. Having surmounted the challenge of gardening and grasped

In no time, the floor space at Home Farm was filled to capacity with everything from old lightning rods to croquet sets and miniature golf flags, to name a fraction of the paraphernalia. Foreseeing that predicament, Marty rigged crosswires to suspend the surplus.

■ *R i g h t :*

While Marty was finishing the roof, Kit busied herself sharpening the picket fence.

■ *B e l o w :*

With a quantity of cats that fluctuates around eight, birdhouses are more ornamental than anything. Still, just in case prospective residents didn't notice the danger, Kit thought it wise to point out the impending problem.

the ropes, they could now play the clowns — and so they did, with a vengeance. Fond of practical jokes, they punctuated their property with an array of suggestive signs that spell out sentiments that most gardeners only mumble under their breath. The first such foray into snide signage came immediately after the tornado, when they stuck FUNERAL PARKING signs around the driveway in a gesture of gallows humor.

Marty and Kit became more dia-

bolical as time went on. You can just see them snickering from the pantry window as they watch visitors wander around and around the property after heeding the PLEASE USE SMALL GATE sign flanking an entry that could easily fit three abreast. They also take glee when innocent victims are tricked by a mirror that renders a fence invisible and makes the garden appear endless.

Everything in the Sagendorf domain is slightly wacky. Flowerpots

forms of miniature myrtles to match the scale of her miniature forcing frames.

Marty pokes fun at her topiary attempts. But he ribs her about everything, from the eight "grumpy old cats" that she's collected to the series of points that cap the garden's fence. "She spent hours sharpening those pickets when I was working on the roof," Marty confides with a wink. "It's true," Kit says. "One false move and he could be compost." ❧

■ *Below:*

Few gardeners have enough time to keep abreast of all the weeding, but Kit is one of those rare, brave souls to turn the error of her ways into a tourist attraction. Or, as Kit puts it, "if you can't beat them, join them."

on the directionals of a weathervane catch the wind and send the contraption whirling around in a frenzy that threatens imminent takeoff. There's a short-necked topiary giraffe that resembles a prehistoric version of the creature, before it evolved to forage from higher branches. When asked why the animal is lacking lengthwise, Kit says only, "I got tired halfway up." She never attempted another life-size version of anything. Instead, she now trains tiny tree

WATERWORKS

THROUGHOUT CIVILIZATION, since the beginning of time, water has been an essential ingredient for gardens. In Oriental gardens, it trips bamboo sticks; it fills moats; and its currents gush from the ever-flowing fonts of dolphins and little Belgian boys.

Persian gardens, I am told, invariably incorporated water. Other cultures followed suit, on the theory that water is essential to all living things — birds bathe in it, bees

Above: VEGETABLE BIRDBATH, CLARKSON GARDEN, CAMBRIDGE, MASSACHUSETTS
Right: EXPECTORATING REPTILES, VIZCAYA, MIAMI, FLORIDA

Garden Whimsy

Mosquito and Pool, Les Quatre Vents, La Malbaie, Quebec

Garden Whimsy

sip it. And anyway, we enjoy its music. Few sounds are as tranquil as the babbling of water over stones or the splashing of a fountain over cement.

The French handled water very well, culminating with the court of Louis XIV but certainly not confined to Versailles. The British were not quite so adept. For many centuries, moats were all they could muster, given the prevailing flat turf.

WATER HAS PROVED A FITTING MEDIUM for practical jokes. Throughout the ages, gardeners have delighted in all sorts of devices that might startle anyone naive enough to walk too far ahead. At Chatsworth, the estate of the duke and duchess of Devonshire and a place of generously flowing moisture, water jets were installed to send streams shooting up the skirts of ladies when they trod on a certain stepping-stone. In the same vein, jets were strategically placed at other junctures in the "pleasure grounds" to hit the guest straight in the eye. I'm not sure whether fun was had by all, but the host reputedly was amused.

For better or worse, water is sufficiently essential to provoke homeowners to hire backhoes and create wetlands where none previously existed, sometimes with disastrous results. After my garden was rototilled, the first element I installed, realizing that water is necessary to any landscape, was an old enamel sink found on the periphery of the property. "My water feature," I declared it, making a solemn promise to the neighbors that further bathroom fixtures would not be forthcoming. ❧

TRYSTS

THE GARDEN IS A SMOLDERING PLACE, what with the love-lies-bleeding draped over the bleeding hearts. Enter at your own risk. Once you brush past the kiss-me-over-the-garden-gate and tiptoe through the love-in-a-mist, anything could happen. 🐚

Left: VERSAILLES, FRANCE   *Above:* GARDEN ORNAMENT SALE, THE COTSWOLDS, ENGLAND

Peter Wooster:
LORD PETER WHIMSY

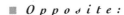

HEN YOU LEAST EXPECT IT, Peter Wooster will come driving up in his 1955 melon-colored pickup and command that you hop in. "The *Sanguisorba menziesii* is in blossom," he'll bellow, "and there isn't a second to lose."

Clutching his "scream bar" for dear life, you bounce up his winding road and come to a screeching halt beside the big yellow garage that he has transformed into his home. You scurry down the field to his garden and spend the next few minutes kneeling in homage in front of a tiny sprawling

 Opposite:

The fact that the garden had to be contained within a fence was something of a saving grace. "It can't expand," proclaimed Peter — and then proceeded to add nursery beds beyond the prescribed limits.

Left:

By midseason, Peter Wooster can easily be obliterated by the undergrowth.

■ The greenhouse has a yard all its own. Like some sort of petrified playground, it is filled with the overflow of succulents in the summer. Anyone brave enough to enter risks being jabbed, poked in the eye, or frisked by the flora.

plant that only a connoisseur could love. Clearly it will remain in flower for the next several weeks, probably the next few months. But Peter's philosophy of life obviously hinges heavily on *carpe diem*.

*I*N PETER'S GARDEN, the six twenty-by-thirty-five-foot rectangular beds, arranged in neat trios on either side of a central meridian, are always meticulously edged to razor sharpness. The grass is sheared to a plush carpet, and the melon-colored pickup is parked where it can conveniently be seen from the Victorian circle in the garden's central aisle. I liken the truck's color to cantaloupe, but Peter calls the hue Velveeta. Perhaps not coincidentally, it always seems to match the flowers at that end of the garden. Although Peter would be the last to admit to it, the pickup has become a garden feature.

"All right," he'll concede, "I guess it could be called an accessory." That's what gardening is all about for Peter Wooster: accessories.

Peter had a 1964 Lincoln conver-

■ The greenhouse is so dense with plants in winter that visitors must take off their overcoats in order to fit through. But when the plants are at "summer camp," it's a whole different scene, with enough open space to serve dinner for eight.

tible and a 1967 Morris Minor when he decided that a 1955 Chevy pickup was just what he needed. Smitten by its "hysterical color" rather than its car-worthiness, he bought it and proceeded to perform a few necessary repairs. He replaced the wiring, fenders, deck, rear end, transmission, tires, windows, locks, and doorknobs. "In short, I replaced the truck," he says, hastening to add, "but at first glance, it was a steal."

THE GARDEN CAME about in very much the same way. It all began thirteen years ago with a wooden gazebo (designed by the famous architect Ehrick Rossiter) that was slated to be tossed from a nearby estate and a one-hundred-foot-square deer fence stranded in the midst of a vast field. That's how it started, but it progressed rapidly and is now a completely different place. First came the structure. At open-air antique sales and flea markets and through dealers who think they've spotted a sucker, Peter acquired a phenomenal array of artifacts. Someone else would stroll right

past that relic of a gate without realizing how pert the crowning finial would look poking above a sea of abutilons and coleus. Any other sensible soul would walk on by the slightly crooked weathervane that now upholds both an ipomoea and a cobaea. The coal scuttle undoubtedly seemed so worthless that he got it for a song. Its gaping barrow now serves as a planter by his door. An orphaned cupola forms a corral, herding the plume poppy so it doesn't encroach on its neighbors.

Those are some of the larger items. But God is in the details, and therefore so is Peter. Gates are topped with wrought-iron archways meant to look like vines, and the latches are just a little out of whack. Fence posts are crowned with a collection of odd finials. And almost everything was obtained for little or nothing. The genius of Peter's garden is not what he's found to fill it with but the cunning applications that he's devised for the assemblage.

The accessories had better be inexpensive, because a lot of capital is invested in plants. Peter presides over what could best be called a botanical

■ *Overleaf:*

English, nineteenth-century, and gorgeous, Peter's sundial presides over the central aisle of the garden with appropriate pomp and ceremony. The only problem is that the gnomon is not proper for this hemisphere. The sundial arrived in April and was dutifully positioned to cast a shadow on the correct marking according to Peter's house clocks (set for split-hair accuracy by Greenwich Mean Time). So for a minute in April Peter's sundial tells time correctly. Every year. If it's sunny.

explains it, the British course is much more convoluted than the American version, "forcing you to bump into your opponent more often."

There's nothing complicated about the design of the garden as a whole. It's a tidy configuration of straight lines and simple geometry. No undulations, no fancy footsteps. There's a reason for that: fathoming the plants takes all your strength.

■ *A b o v e :*

Peter's garden might be a free-for-all, but he did install stakes of recycled junipers for the honeysuckle to mount to define boundaries.

■ *R i g h t :*

Even the containers are a triumphant jumble, albeit masterfully composed, such as this symphony in phormium, tolmeia, and tweedia.

zoo. Although the layout is simple, the inventory is mind-boggling. And eclectic. Besides the rarity-rich beds and borders, the garden features a Belgian fence underplanted with species crocus and other minor bulbs; a Victorian circle; a gazebo with begonias beneath; and a baptismal font that serves as a scree for alpines. There are some cold frames and holding beds off to one side, and a greenhouse with a rather zany fenced succulent garden on another side. Beyond the greenhouse are a lily pond and a croquet lawn. The lawn's design is dictated by the British regulations because, as Peter

"The theme of the garden is 'Every man for himself,'" Peter says, referring to the seeming free-for-all in each rectangular bed. In fact, though, Peter is continually digging plants up to maintain discipline. The spoils are divided and given to fledgling gardeners. However he does it, the garden doesn't strike you as a hodgepodge. Instead, it's punctuated by ingenious combinations, which Peter explains away as "happy accidents."

"When you try to compose a color scheme, it's doomed. It looks abysmal. When you arbitrarily jam everything together, great flirtations are bound to happen." In Peter's mélange, everything synchronizes; even volunteers seemingly self-sow where they can be seen to best advantage. "Except the sunflowers," Peter interjects. "They always come up in exactly the wrong place."

Of course, not everything works. Peter opens his garden occasionally for tours, and a terrible rainstorm hit the day before one such opening. Peter called to say that he was on the couch, "in the fetal position," fearful of the consequences while all hell broke loose outdoors. The next day actually found the garden in fairly decent condition after a few hours of raking and deadheading — except for the 'Annabelle' hydrangea. Since "it required four thousand sticks to hold up the drenched oversize heads," it was removed.

Oh, well. With the wisdom of a Buddhist monk seeking enlightenment, Peter sees his garden as a journey. As he wrote in a Garden Conservancy Open Days Directory, "The garden shows no signs of settling down. The cotinus has the 'crud.' Moles ate the *Senecio doria*, and the hollyhocks have rust. But we try." ❧

■ If a planting doesn't dwarf its point of origin, then it hasn't succeeded in Peter's eyes.

THE BORROWED LANDSCAPE

JUST AS THE JAPANESE PERFECTED THE ART of incorporating distant vistas into their small back yards, adding extraneous objects to your own scene must be done with panache. To accent the majesty of far-off hills, the Japanese often harness the gentle arch of a tree limb or a cloud of nearby azalea blossoms. But anything can be part of a garden if it's skillfully parked and framed to best advantage. 🐌

Above: 1946 DODGE, HYLL GARDEN, BANTAM, CONNECTICUT
Right: 1955 CHEVY, WOOSTER GARDEN, ROXBURY, CONNECTICUT

Moses Pendleton:

THE *Sunflower* SAGA

ON'T VISIT Moses Pendleton in August. It just isn't prudent to set foot on his property during the throes of the annual sunflower fiasco. Moses doesn't suffer any sort of failure lightly, and he finds helianthus-related humiliations particularly hard to bear.

By profession Moses Pendleton is a choreographer, the cofounder of the dance troupe Pilobolus and the current artistic director for Momix, a troupe that combines gymnastic feats with dance movement. Yet flowers, especially sunflowers, aren't too far off the beaten track of his career. By Moses' definition, nature and growth — a blossom unfolding and a sprout stretching toward the light — can be expressed in a few deft movements of the human body. They're inspiration. But it's more than that. Somewhere in Moses' rather unique set of synapses, sunflowers equal sexuality, reproduction, and energy. So they always seem to worm their way into his dances. Back when things were going smoothly, you could find Moses at the center of his sunflower garden every morning, getting "energized." "I'm a solarist," he once quipped. "The sunflowers are like desk lamps, and I worship them." For Moses, these plants are like spades or trowels: they're tools.

Moses found these tools twenty years ago, when he moved to a cavernous Victorian house in rural western Connecticut. It didn't take him long to realize that the house needed

■ *Opposite:*

In past years, the sunflower maze led to a table set with a feast for sixty. But recently, something more macabre seemed appropriate.

something lapping around its ankles. For someone who is rather fond of quirkiness and has no qualms about instant gratification, sunflowers are just the ticket. You plant the seeds, you watch them grow, and in a few brief months you enjoy lots of big — very big — cheerful yellow blossoms.

*M*OSES ISN'T PRONE to doing anything by halves, so he planted a gigantic wheel, one hundred feet in diameter, with six spokes of densely packed sunflowers. Nothing if not a party animal, he used the sunflower extravaganza to provoke soirees with flowing wine, nearly naked bodies flitting among the foliage, and a table for sixty set at the center. The soirees were the talk of the town; big names vied for a place on the A list, and paparazzi lurked in the shrubbery trying to catch a celebrity or two in a compromising moment. As I hear it, there was plenty of opportunity.

The parties were fun, to be sure, but the sunflowers earned their keep for more practical purposes. The gargantuan, radiantly colored botanical overachievers inspired choreography, costumes, and videos. On more than one occasion, those XXL flowers were strategically placed in lieu of fig leaves. A few well-positioned 'Mammoth Russians' could keep even the most modest of audiences in the dark.

Word spread. In fact, anyone who set foot in Moses' house expected to see sunflowers. And he didn't disappoint. The biggest sunflower ("Miss Sunflower 1989" or "Miss Sunflower 1991") was selected and displayed prominently in the foyer. Every rocking chair on the front porch had a rather macabre sunflower-faced scarecrow stationed on its cushions, every room in the house was haunted by "double headers" and other floral freaks, and sunflower heads instead of family portraits were pinned to the wallpaper lining the stairs. At Christmas, the hearth mantel was strewn with helianthus rather than pine cones or evergreens.

PERHAPS there is something slightly warped about worshipping one flower as your heart's sole desire. Nature seems to shy away from a monogamous relationship. For whatever reason, Moses' sunflowers became elusive, with the problems going far beyond the predators that had once plagued the sunflower field. First it was verticillium wilt; then it was rhizoctonia compounded by a bevy of other opportunistic viruses. Initially a single plant here and there curled up its leaves and passed on to helianthus heaven. Then stems started succumbing wholesale to a white mold. Before long, the mortality rate was 90 percent or more. "Instead of going down to the garden to become inspired, I went down to bury the dead," Moses moans. "It was like a hazardous waste dump or a murder scene. I was tempted to string up yellow police barrier tape." There was no known cure, and the epidemic showed no signs of abating on its own.

Moses tried everything. He altered his planting pattern to leave infected soil fallow; he spaced the plants so each had plenty of breathing room; he burned infected bedfellows. Tools that came in contact with diseased plants were sterilized. He sprayed every seven to ten days with an antifungal spray, stopping short only of applying anything that required a "zoot suit" to protect the applicator. He sought alternatives. He began experimenting with cultivars other than 'Mammoth Russian', which remains his heartthrob. Every extension agent and university botanist who would listen to his plight was consulted.

Just as he has for twenty years, Moses Pendleton threw a sunflower party this summer. But this year the feast was held after dark and the garden was not illuminated. If you squinted and didn't examine the scene too closely, you couldn't tell that many of the sunflowers were propped-up corpses rather than healthy plants. Others had been watered heavily to counteract wilt just before company arrived. As for Moses, he did his best to keep up appearances. "But really," he confided, "I'm in mourning."

Moses is an optimist; he has never lost faith. And I've heard he put in an order for sunflower seeds for next season. ❧

THE CUTTING EDGE

I'M NOT THE FIRST TO LOOK ASKANCE at yew trees shaped into turtledoves. Throughout history, topiary has elicited mixed reactions. There are those who look at a boxwood and think "giraffe," and there are those who prefer it left free-form. The argument has been batted back and forth for a few centuries.

Although topiary is the latest and hottest fad, there's nothing new about pruning plants into whimsical forms. The ancient Greeks reputedly inaugurated the practice of shearing shrubs into shapes. Thanks to Cneus Matius, a friend of Julius Caesar's and a champion of *topiarius*, the Romans followed suit, and the art proliferated well into medieval times. In more recent history, when man began to ponder such things, he proceeded to ask whether it was proper to take such license. Was the privet meant to look like a peacock? Was it right to coax the boxwood to resemble a teapot?

In the eighteenth century, two satirists and onetime friends, Alexander Pope and Joseph Addison, agreed on only one thing: that topiary was "a monument to perverted taste." Crusading to quell a trend that threatened to take over the landscape with verdant fowl and fauna, Pope wrote: "A citizen is no sooner proprietor of a couple of yews, but he entertains thoughts of erecting them into giants. I know an eminent cook, who beautified his country seat with a coronation dinner in greens, where you see the champion flourishing on horseback at one end of the table, and the queen in perpetual youth at the other."

Part of the lure is the challenge. Heaven knows, creating Adam, Eve, and the serpent in juniper is no easy feat. First of all, logistics and light must be

Left: CORKSCREW CYPRESSES, NEWTON VINEYARDS, ST. HELENA, CALIFORNIA

This page and following spread: THE ZOO GARDEN, GREEN ANIMALS, PORTSMOUTH, RHODE ISLAND

considered. Wind coming from one side of a topiary will totally defeat the symmetry, and sun cannot easily penetrate the underbelly of a green elephant. Or the legs, for that matter. So, infantile though the finished form might look, it takes a bit of doing to make an oversize Peter Rabbit.

SOMETHING WITHIN ME loves a good chess piece carved out of yew or a setting hen sculpted of juniper. Something in my heart leaps when I encounter a cleverly clipped hunt scene, hounds and horsemen in hot pursuit of the fox. But then, I'm also fond of nursery rhymes and Saturday-morning cartoons. Lord Bacon saw the connection clearly. Writing in Shakespearean times, he proclaimed, "I for my part do not like images cut in juniper or other garden stuff; they be for children." Lord Bacon was not one to throw stones, however. In describing the estate of his fondest dreams, he wrote that it was surrounded by a garden enclosed in an arched hedge. Not just any arched hedge — his had turrets. And over every turret, "a cage of birds . . . and over every space between the arches some other little figure." My thoughts precisely — bring on the teddy bears. ❧

Garden Whimsy

VI.

Bunny Williams:
Designs on Nature

UNNY WILLIAMS'S FIRST stab at gardening on her Connecticut property was planting vegetables. "You can only have finite fun in the perennial garden," she explains. It's true. Things remain fairly static in a perennial display. By con-trast, in the potager, everything is tossed up in the air at regular intervals. Another chapter starts every few months, as new crops fill positions vacated by previous performers that have been harvested for the table. The show must go on, even if the former prima donnas are now compost.

■ *Opposite:*

Bunny readily admits that the vegetable garden could easily overtake her entire property, so she's thankful that woods form a boundary on one end and the carriage shed impedes progress on the other.

■ *Left:*

Bona fide chickens are not welcome in the vegetable garden. Cement replicas wreak less havoc.

79

■ Bunny's vegetable garden is mobile. Not only are the beds subject to harvest on a regular basis, but the "imported talent" of potted argyranthemums, heliotrope, and scented-leaf geraniums is enlisted whenever a spark of color is required.

Bunny admits, however, that the vegetable garden wasn't an instant success story. As she describes it, some gardeners have beginner's luck, but her first few sunny seasons were spent groping in the dark. The place demanded a garden; that fact was immediately self-evident. And Bunny saw good reason for the garden in question to be amply stocked with homegrown food. "So we plowed up a space and put in some tomatoes and squash. It was truly ugly," she says of those initial attempts. Inspiration proved evasive for a few floundering years, until she beheld her first ornamental vegetable garden. The chemistry was strong. She liked the food, she liked the setting, but best of all she liked the accouterments. As Bunny is the first to confess, "A lot of people begin gardening because they're fascinated by horticulture, but I'm transfixed by edging tiles."

That admission comes as no surprise to anyone who knows Bunny Williams. She is a partner in the Manhattan garden antique shop Treillage as well as an interior designer of renown. However, it's entirely possible to meet the serious side of Bunny in the city and fail to realize that she harbors a satirical bent. Beneath it all, she craves levity. "It's crucial — in a garden as well as in a relationship. Humor sees you through anything." The potager allowed Bunny to enjoy a field day on a continual basis.

It could be said that the whimsy of Bunny's potager lies in the fact that it's not purely for vegetables. Furthermore, it utilizes ornaments that are not seen strictly as garden fodder. It's the Lewis Carroll version of a vegetable garden — observed through the looking glass, with everything slightly askew. Bulbs start the season, but their heads are chopped off for bouquets. Later on come loads of blossoms (the inedible contingent), nearly smothering the more practical leafy greens. If this is a

■ **Every room needs the proper furnishings.**

Bunny wonders why she tolerates the ruckus that the woodsman creates as his squeaky joints saw, but he serves his purpose, and she figures that he'll fall apart sooner or later. "The beauty of wooden art is that it can be counted on not to last forever," she says.

vegetable garden, it is certainly a boisterous version. To prevent the slightest lull, potted plants crowd the aisles like a conquering army storming the home battlements. "The beauty of the vegetable garden is that if you hate something," Bunny says, "you just plow it under." Indeed.

*T*HE PLANTS are only part of it. Treillage is filled with things that require what I call "vision" for their possibilities to be recognized. Even at that, sometimes it seems as though Bunny saves the most visionary pieces for her own back yard. At least, the potager features many objects that undoubtedly required some elbow grease, polish, and a management-level position in the right setting to shine.

The focal point is a nineteenth-century lightning rod (found at a flea market) set fashionably akimbo. Its placement is no happenstance. "Anything with a square pattern needs an anchor in the middle," proclaims the interior designer. Turned finials add swank to a weathered barnyard fence. And in keeping with the farm theme, the garden is guarded by a flock of stone chickens. Ironically, the cackle of bona fide resident hens (Black Polish, Rhode Island Reds, Plymouth Rocks, and Bantams) can be heard drifting from over yonder. But the genuine articles are not permitted within the potager premises, because Bunny is bent on reaping what she sows.

Also for reasons of preserving the produce of the garden, and long before anyone was collecting whirligigs, Bunny installed a rather mean-spirited woodsman sawing logs. He looks about as friendly as your average Dutch uncle, and since his mechanisms are never properly oiled, he squeaks in the slightest breeze. Beyond driving Bunny bats, the commotion scares the crows, preventing fowl play, so to speak.

There are cloches, forcers, tepees, and all sorts of sticks placed unceremoniously where they can support vines or floppy stems. There's an arbor in the shade and étagères with battalions of little pots basking in the sun. It's bucolic gone to finishing school, but still playing pranks in the dormito-

ry. And given such a bounty of paraphernalia, the scene could easily look like a menagerie, except for the unifying saving grace: the brick walks and edged beds that give everything a sense of importance. That's the secret.

The potager is no longer the only garden on the rustic eleven-acre grounds. Although the rest of the property is more formal, tongue-in-cheek humor infiltrates the fringes. The back steps leading down to the perennial garden are guarded by a pair of cowardly lions, grinning and pawing cement balls; the swimming pool features an urn sprouting a blooming aloe where the diving board would normally be, and huge Italian pots spill with nothing more formal than a tangled mass of jocular, saucy-faced pansies.

You have to be brave. Even Bunny confesses that sometimes it works, sometimes it doesn't. "One year," she says, "I looked out and realized that the garden was adorned in the world's worst color combination. If I did that in somebody's house, I'd be shot." ❧

■ Other areas of Bunny's garden give a nod to formality. Although the huge terracotta pots lining the back terrace hold nothing fancier than pansies, standard *Convolvulus cneorum* flank the playful lions.

OF MICE AND MEN

THE WAY I SEE IT, two forces are at work in any garden. There are the people, laying designs on grid paper, balancing heights and shapes, arranging complementary colors and textures, orchestrating a flowing progression from the earliest blooming date until the fading of the last rose of summer. And then, working with equally concerted effort, there are the animals. The animals are also intent on their strategies, deciding what should grow where — and what shouldn't be in the garden at all.

According to my theory, every animal has its own vision of how the ideal garden should look. Voles believe that all the bulbs ought to be rearranged; rabbits feel that lettuce should be thinned out considerably. Deer maintain that all the plants should be eradicated. Given this, I'm fascinated by the prevalence of lion statues guarding gardens. Because lions, of course, are convinced that the world should harbor no gardeners at all.

Left: FOO LION, NARA, JAPAN
Above: GATEKEEPERS, NEWTON VINEYARDS, ST. HELENA, CALIFORNIA
Right: BOWLING LION, WILLIAMS GARDEN, FALLS VILLAGE, CONNECTICUT

FOLLIES

THE BEAUTY OF THE IMAGINATION is that it's so easily stretched. If you've already created a scene that pushes the boundaries of reality, well, why not embroider on that suspension? That's how follies came about. By the fifteenth century, Italian architecture was already laden with loggias, galleries, trompe l'oeil, and other arguably artificial elements. It was just a step outside to the garden.

So we have Italy to blame for the grottoes, temples, mazes, pavilions, ruined castles, caverns, crumbling bridges, and fake waterfalls that were sprouting in gardens by the seventeenth century. It was the Italians, with their fertile sense of drama, who built elaborate structures dedicated to mythical creatures and gods and goddesses. And wouldn't you know it, the ardent Italians created sumptuous garden pavilions far off the beaten track, to lure innocent wanderers, to set the mood, to foster seduction. It was all based on romance.

But it wasn't always laughter and gaiety. An innocent pedestrian in the woods might be startled by a contorted hell's mask hidden in a thicket. A cave could be guarded by a seething monster or a grotesque gaping mouth. The garden wasn't necessarily a beautiful place or a joyous place, but it was an adventure. It held intrigue.

In the eighteenth and nineteenth centuries, other Europeans built their own versions of follies. Not quite as hot-blooded as the Italians, they based follies on fable rather than ardor, floating Bacchus in ponds or creating fountains à la Aesop. The element of surprise was strong, the jest was the thing. But follies still had a strong dreamlike quality.

Although present-day follies tend not to be gilded or as elaborate as they were when, say, the Sun King reigned, they can still be found. Whenever you paint a trompe l'oeil or accent a spit of land with a pavilion, you're harking back to the ancient tradition.

There are as many different sorts of follies as imagination will create, from eight-foot gazing balls to mirrors that reflect the garden. They can be stately or crumbled, constructed of stone or of seashells, set proudly at the promontory of a hill, or secreted in the woods. Follies have only one thing in common: each and every one is an illusion. ৵

THE GREAT MASK, GIARDINI GIUSTI, VERONA, ITALY

Jana Drobinsky:
Time Capsule

JANA OLSON DROBINSKY'S earliest memories are of playing in mud holes and tree houses. "I was a farm kid," she explains. "I made fairy houses in the crevices of hollow trees and went around digging up cow bones to decorate them. I collected bottle caps to pave the entryways . . . Never told the neighbors about it, though." And that was a good thing, because Jana grew up in Minnesota,

■ *Opposite:*

Somehow the "space alien milieu" of *Echium wildpretii* appealed to Jana. It didn't seem entirely foreign to her place, either.

■ *Left:*

One summer Jana handed a friend a spool of wire and challenged him to produce a gate. The result proved even crazier than she'd expected.

■ *O v e r l e a f :*
Texture is everything
when creating something
that resembles a moon
surface.

where they don't mess around with their cow bones.

In contrast, Berkeley is a place of an entirely different color. "First of all, you've got to understand that lawn is not king here," she says, launching into her short monologue on how the San Francisco Bay area differs from the Upper Midwest. "Only five things

grew in Minnesota, and two of them were junipers," she explains. "When I came to California, I was thrilled by the lack of convention. You can't grow grass here, so the average garden is a pile of weeds. People might do some tidying up, but that's it." As for herself, Jana shrugs her shoulders. "I just do things for fun."

Although Jana insists that the garden isn't dedicated solely to recycling, she's proud when she can find a purpose for something discarded — like manhole covers.

HE DOES SEEM TO have a good time. Although her first substantial Berkeley garden comprised less than a quarter of an acre, it packed considerable punch. When she and her husband moved into what she calls "the boring little house" not far from the heart of the city, she was in no rush to fix up the yard immediately. "It took us two years to unpack our stuff," she recounts. They spent some time working on the

■ When Jana Drobinsky incorporates strong colors, she doesn't limit herself solely to plants. Meanwhile, a fence kept out pests when the corgi became too corpulent to patrol the premises.

house, "but when we were finished, it was still a nondescript bungalow."

Although work on the yard took some time getting under way, the garden was imbued with a theme when it finally jelled. In Jana's word, it was an expression of "upheaval." Or, to be more explicit, "It was earthquake geology. It was my interpretation of the crusted layers that might be exposed if the earth moved, revealing an era in Berkeley's evolution." Precisely what era did she have in mind, I can't help but ask. "The Hedonistic Era," she responds without hesitation.

*H*OW DID I GUESS? Could it have been the stratum of champagne bottles embedded in the soil bottoms up? Or maybe the other debris scattered about? Succulents spewed from clay sewer pipes, and the meadow garden could be navigated only by steppingstones made of manhole covers. "I'm often described as someone who scrounges recycled materials and then puts them to constructive employment, but that's not what this is really all about," confides Jana. What is it about, then? "It's art," she says.

One can't help but wonder what gave her the idea in the first place. "It was the rocks," she explains. "We have this wonderful multicolored volcanic rock here; that was the guiding principle. I matched the plants to the rocks to give a rainbow effect. And then we were fortunate to be blessed by all that broken concrete from the driveway we tore up . . ." Obviously, it was a happening just waiting to be hatched.

The recycled materials were only part of it. They just enhanced the plants, which could only be called eye-popping. "I like strong colors," says Jana, expressing the obvious. Apparently she's also fond of plants of inventive form and texture. The result was that the whole place resembled a moonscape.

Now the Drobinskys are moving to a place with more room to fiddle around. Mum's the word about the theme of Jana's future garden. As with the previous one, she's waiting for the place to speak to her. Heaven knows what it will say this time. ☙

■ *L e f t :*

Unfortunately, Jana's corgi passed on "to his richer rewards" recently.

CHEAP LABOR

HUMANITY IS FOREVER SEEKING APPLICATIONS, and that might explain why we feel sure animals should serve some useful purpose in the garden. The cat should control moles; the dog ought to deter deer. But the fact is, they don't. The cat scares off songbirds (if it doesn't kill them), or it finds a shady corner, stretches out, and crushes the flowers. The dog excavates burrows that have nothing to do with predators and tramples paths where you didn't intend to have an access road. Lizards should eat pests but spend their days frightening visitors instead; peacocks peck the wrong seedlings, and chickens scratch where they shouldn't. Rabbits nibble fresh young leaves and lead the dog on a merry chase. None of them do the work that they were detailed to accomplish. The truth is that animals, domestic or otherwise, are botanically counterproductive. From a horticultural standpoint, the only safe pet is made of cement. 🐾

Left: CHARLIE,
ROONEY GARDEN,
MIDDLEBURY,
VERMONT

Right: BLACKIE,
DOWNTOWN ELY
GARDENS,
ELY, VERMONT

Above: WINSTON, SAGENDORF GARDEN, BRIDGEWATER, CONNECTICUT

Right: WOODY, MOIR GARDEN, LYME, NEW HAMPSHIRE

Alice Moir:

Granny's Garden

ALICE MOIR CLAIMS THAT SHE threw horticultural caution to the wind for the sole purpose of pleasing her grandchildren. But don't believe a word of it. A folk artist by profession, Alice was actually entertaining herself when she filled her garden with sever-al dozen birdhouses, and she was indulging her own sense of quirkiness when she set up the garden's focal point. Some of us might stand in the middle of the rectangular beds and wonder aloud about the logic of accenting the scene with a makeshift cardboard sundial. Time is fleeting, so

■ *Opposite:*

When asked to describe their granny's garden, Alice's grandchildren have been overheard to explain that she's planted "more birdhouses than flowers."

■ *Left:*

Alice Moir spends long winters doing crewel work, and Genesis was a common theme of early patterns. "Except Eve and Adam were more clothed back then," she says. She did a more liberal version for the garden.

The garden came complete with picket fence, which now serves as a retirement community for what Alice calls her "holey gloves."

why should a timepiece last forever?

The sundial was a joke, of course, as was the chair with caning in such a deteriorated state that it was of no earthly good for its proper function. But Alice saw an application. In its retirement, the chair was stationed over the iris bed. The stalks poke through the seat and thus require no further staking against the winds that gust from the river.

THE BACK YARD started seriously enough, with eight raised beds that Alice and her husband, Bill, inherited from a previous owner of the riverside house in northern New England. In its past life, it was a vegetable garden positioned strategically at the only place on the steep hill where you could effectively cultivate vegetables. Alice converted it into an herb garden, and herbs still maintain a predominant presence. But now other members of the botanical kingdom have settled in as well. ("Including weeds," Alice says. "There's no point in being fanatical about this sort of thing.")

Every year the garden gets a new array of accouterments, such as another garden seat that no one can use because it's firmly encased in a tangle of vines. Tarnished artifacts, like a wheelbarrow with an old cider barrel set on top, meant to look like a mobile watering unit, are everywhere, beginning with the newest

addition to the scene. In the front yard, gazing into the dining room picture window, the larger-than-life classical Four Seasons statues — a waif lugging an armload of wood for winter, a lass clutching a bunch of flowers for spring, a maiden carrying wheat for summer, and a gentle-woman toting grapes for fall — are dressed with an outer layer of local college mufflers and beanies. Farther down toward the river, a garishly painted gingerbread playhouse has a garden of its own — with wooden flowers, which Alice installed because wooden tulips are "the only plant that young children are capable of nurturing."

■ *Opposite:*

Naturally, the preponderance of birdhouses attracted other parties.

■ *Above:*

The rarely occupied garden bench finally became an "honorary chair" for scholarly endeavors.

■ *Left:*

Since sandpipers are scarce in Hanover, New Hampshire, Alice decided to take matters into her own hands.

ANY OF ALICE'S ideas have been imported from other places. From Charleston she got a joggling board that bounces visitors up and down and delivers wonderful breezes up their skirt, if they happen to be wearing a skirt. Her best idea came from a town near London, where she encountered signs on garden gates advertising the opening of a private garden. GARDEN OPEN TODAY, the signs read, and visitors could walk about in it. If you were lucky, you could find someone to ask questions of, and maybe even receive answers from. Alice brought the idea home. On certain days she now hangs a sign informing neighbors that they can come and stroll in her garden. In keeping with the spirit of the event, she puts out another invitation: CRITICISM WELCOME, her sign says. ❧

■ Alice's birdhouse is an exact replica of her own, scaled down.

■ *L e f t :*

From its inception, Alice's garden had a sign that proclaimed it as granny's garden. But the grandchildren added their two cents after the garden was featured in several national magazines.

■ *O v e r l e a f :*

Hoping to instill a love of gardening but savvy about a grandchild's sense of responsibility, Alice chose wooden flowers as the safest route.

the
Secret
Garden

FOR THE BIRDS

ARDENERS RULE THEIR domains with a controlling hand, inviting only certain species to live there. As evidence, I submit the fact that we never encounter raccoon sheds or mole parlors. It's an ill-concealed fact that the cozy places gardeners install for slugs are actually traps meant to lure them in, intoxicate them, and drown them. Lures for Japanese beetles do not have the insects' comfort or well-being in mind.

Birds, however, are welcome in the garden, so we gardeners put up birdhouses. With the exception of crows and grackles, we don't really care what moves in, as long as it's feathered. Even if the residents gobble up all our earthworms, we don't grumble, as long as they sing and diminish the grub population.

My fear is that birdhouses will begin to lack any raison d'être at all. Just as women stumble around in stiletto heels and carpenters build houses with cupboard doors that can't possibly be opened, the birdhouses of the future will not be fit housing for any feathered visitor. They will be art, but they'll be empty nests.

Left: BIRD COTTAGE,
AZARIAN GARDEN,
PLAINFIELD, VERMONT

Above: MARTEN HOUSE,
DEAL GARDEN,
FRIENDSHIP, MAINE

NO BIRDS

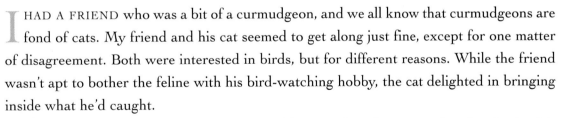

MY GARDEN once contained a bird-house. It was designed for blue-birds, constructed and positioned carefully according to the recommendations of the Audubon folks — facing southeast, four feet above the ground, and several miles from the nearest neighboring bluebird house. Amazingly, a bluebird took an interest — I caught sight of a male checking it out one day in early April. He seemed to find it well enough to his liking. In fact, he returned with the wife a few hours later, and she started furnishing. I thought we would all enjoy connubial bliss, until my Maine coon cat happened along . . .

I HAD A FRIEND who was a bit of a curmudgeon, and we all know that curmudgeons are fond of cats. My friend and his cat seemed to get along just fine, except for one matter of disagreement. Both were interested in birds, but for different reasons. While the friend wasn't apt to bother the feline with his bird-watching hobby, the cat delighted in bringing inside what he'd caught.

My friend was a forthright man, a fellow of few words and strong action. I arrived at his house one day to find a brass plaque neatly affixed to the front door, at just about eye level for a cat. In the shiny surface of the brass the words were succinctly engraved: NO BIRDS.

Left: BIRD CONDO, HYLL GARDEN, BANTAM, CONNECTICUT
Above: BIRCH BIRDHOUSE, ELYE GARDEN, WILLIAMSVILLE, NEW YORK

Shepherd Ogden:
Tossed Salad

SHEPHERD OGDEN WAS ambivalent about flaunting his family in public. "You'll have to ask Ellen if you can use pictures of the kids in your book," he explained. "I can't expose my women to the world without their permission, you know. I'm supposed to keep them cloistered, like fine wine." Of course, permission was immediately granted when I applied to Shepherd's wife, Ellen. When he heard the news, Shep breathed an audible sigh of relief, feigning fear of his petite partner. "She's very strong, you know," he confided, and then pro-

■ *Opposite:*

During her daughter Molly's tea-party phase, Ellen knew just where to find her when it came time to harvest.

■ *Left:*

There was no question that Shep's garden would be organic — he is the grandson of Samuel R. Ogden, Sr., a famous early advocate of organic gardening.

gardener in residence, and a rather successful one at that. But it didn't start that way. At first Shep was a starving artist. Then he graduated to struggling poet. Ellen figures she's hit upon the reason that he made a go of gardening. "When Shep proposed, he told my father that he would support me on lettuce," she explains, "and Shep can never lose a bet."

Shep was plying Ellen with greens long before the garden was planted, in 1980. From subsistence

ceeded to tell tales of how she hauled sheetrock single-handedly when the house was being built. "That sheetrock weighs at least a hundred pounds," he pointed out, "and Ellen weighs less."

Shep, Ellen, and their children tend a vegetable plot in Londonderry, Vermont, loosely described by Shep as "Vermont funky formal" — the only formality being the sharp-lined, crisp-cornered organization of the neatly weeded beds. Ellen is the consummate cook, while Shep is the

■ Children have the clearest view of gardening, I think. Unfettered by the laws of nature, unrestricted by the bounds of frost dates or climatic concerns, they go straight for the goal. One very young friend had a particularly good idea. "Let's go out," she suggested, "and plant peanut butter and jelly sandwiches."

At least ten different kinds of sunflowers go into the garden annually, "but they all began as a deeply concerted effort to hide a junk truck," Shep divulges.

farmers they became truck farmers, opening a farm stand and eventually supplying restaurants. Finally they went national and launched the Cook's Garden, the country's first gourmet mail-order seed company. A trial garden was sorely needed, especially the kind that customers might find enjoyable. When the Ogdens took down the greenhouses in front of their house, the only flat expanse on the property suddenly became available, and the vegetable garden was born.

FROM ITS BEGINNING, the vegetable garden has featured its fair share of potatoes, peppers, flowers, and parody. It's a lighthearted affair, but probing Shep about the particulars of the humor is futile. As far as he's concerned, a tongue-in-cheek garden is serious business. He takes the no-nonsense approach to whimsy.

Shep sees himself as a freedom fighter of sorts, liberating the vegetable garden from its burden of practicality. I committed the grievous error of attributing to him the original concept of incorporating ornamental ele-

■ Everyone gets involved in the garden. In fact, Molly (holding Henrietta, her Barred Rock) and her brother, Sam, eventually earned a garden of their own. "And we never tell them what to plant," claims Shep, although vegetables are encouraged.

ments into vegetable beds, but he wouldn't hear of it. "I've been alive only since 1949," he says, "and ornamental vegetable gardening has been practiced since 1500. You can make the presumption that I started the trend, if you wish, but I couldn't in all modesty make the claim myself."

CCORDING TO SHEP, vegetables have been in serious trouble for some decades now. It was the Victory Gardens of World War II that did them in. "Victory Gardens made vegetable gardening into an obligation and a chore," he claims. The cabbage patch was stuffed discreetly behind the garage, with all the other service-oriented aspects of living. "Those gardens," Shep points out, "had no connection with our own sensuality."

Shep is trying to undo all that — or, as he puts it, "We're trying to reunite the pleasurable and the practical." His garden is a place of beauty, infused with the "breath of art." Art is in the family genes, along with a heavy helping of Yankee ingenuity. "My father was a sculptor, and Ellen's grandmother was an art director for the Meredith magazines; both were gardeners," he explains. Obviously, the Ogden beds have roots that aren't altogether in compost.

That would also explain why flowers are sprinkled liberally everywhere, especially the sorts of blossoms that children might adore. "There's a commonality between flowers and vegetables," declares Shep. At the Cook's Garden, that translates into quantities of sunflowers, cosmos, marigolds, sweet peas, and hollyhocks sharing the same raised beds that harbor chartreuse-headed 'Minaret' broccoli, 'Carouby de Maussane' edible-pod peas, 'Wampum' ornamental corn, and strawberry popcorn.

Since I figure that the closest ocean must be several hundred miles from Londonderry, I can't help inquiring about the playhouse — a stately child-size lighthouse (with widow's walk and all) standing sentinel in the garden. Shep can explain, at length. Ellen is of seafaring blood; her family's is a well-known name on Cape Cod. "In fact, when we were married, we had to fish Ellen's family wedding gown out of the

■ Shep describes a farmer's day as "from first bird-chirp in the morning to rototilling with the headlights after dark," which might explain why he gave up the farmstand in favor of a mail-order gourmet seed catalogue. It made for a happier existence.

Provincetown Museum," he says. The family acts as guardians of a scenic old lighthouse in Chatham. The scaled-down replica of that landmark that stands in the vegetable garden was a gift from Ellen's parents, who wanted to give the children a sense of their heritage as well as a place to play.

The garden also harbors gourd birdhouses (or "gourdian angels"), arbors, seats, and a huge boulder in the middle that defied removal (if you can't budge 'em, incorporate 'em). The fence is picket on one side and stockade on the other. It's funky, to be sure. But don't try to bait Shep into admitting that the barrier is bedded in any-

thing but pure logic. Protecting lilacs and blueberries from northwest winter winds on one side and permitting the ingress of summer breezes along the lower border is what the fence is all about. No caprice is intended.

"What I'm trying to do," Shep explains, "is to give back flexibility in the vegetable garden, to expand the portfolio of plants and free them from the tyranny of practicality." A sideways glance from Ellen and the fact that dinner appears to be ready prompt him to nip his lecture in the bud. While setting the table, he says, "That's just a highfalutin way of saying that we're just trying to have fun." ❧

STRANGE BEDFELLOWS

YOU NEVER KNOW WHAT you'll bump into in the garden. Most often it will be whippets, bunnies, Saint Francis of Assisi, or the Four Seasons. Sometimes you run into Mercury, Neptune, Diana, the Muses, or the Philosophers, or perhaps Buddha or the Madonna. But there is the occasional surprise: a five-hundred-times-times-larger-than-life baseball mitt (at Wave Hill, near Yankee Stadium), perhaps, or the Trojan Horse. Raging boars, confrontational goats, and menacing lions all present a kind of surprise — they're meant to startle you — but sluggish tortoises are not unheard of, either.

In the eighteenth and nineteenth centuries you might have found Pan loitering somewhere in the landscape. Throughout the same eras, Venus was often in the garden. Nowadays, metal or bronze insects often hover around, as if the genuine articles weren't bad enough. By the same token, statues of fairies and leprechauns are greeted with mixed emotions. Some statues are meant to make us feel good about ourselves. That's probably what Venus is all about. It *is* consoling, especially at the beginning of the season, before we've shed our winter baggage, to encounter the occasional corpulent naked lady in the undergrowth.

Besides strange creatures and odd characters, other objects sometimes turn up amid the greenery. Gardeners may be forgiven their penchant for urns overflowing with flowers. It's an obvious fit. And where else but outdoors

Left: THE SULTAN, VIRGINIA HOUSE, RICHMOND, VIRGINIA

Right: GHOSTS, BLASS GARDEN, NEW PRESTON, CONNECTICUT

Garden Whimsy

would you place a sundial? In other instances, gardeners merely make good use of found objects — spare baptismal fonts, saddle stones, wagon wheels, and truck tires immediately come to mind.

Statues, I've been told, serve a specific function in the garden. Gargoyles and lions, for instance, make perfect guards at the gates. Once you get past them, other, more user-friendly statues direct the flow of traffic and give the garden a sense of movement, acting as focal points, centering your attention where it should fall, steering you away from the darker edges and the places that haven't yet been weeded. It has also been suggested that statues are tour guides, leading you on. But I wonder, do tour guides lead you on or send you running?

Left: TURTLE AND SNAIL,
LES QUATRE VENTS,
LA MALBAIE, QUEBEC

Right: CIGAR STORE INDIAN,
SCHOELLKOPF GARDEN,
WASHINGTON, CONNECTICUT

Jane Howard Hammerstein:
In *L*IVING COLOR

IF JANE HOWARD HAMMERSTEIN'S garden cannot be detected from the road, it's for good reason. Her strategy is to hide her bits of bravery in back to protect the sensibilities of her easily ruffled Litchfield County neighbors. The neighborhood is, shall we say, subdued, and nobody ever explained to the busy screenwriter and wife of William Hammerstein (eldest son of Oscar Hammerstein, of Rodgers and Hammerstein celebrity) that screaming orange does not belong beside aubergine and raspberry. Or if someone did confide such knowledge, she obviously turned a deaf ear.

■ *Opposite:*

When left to its own devices, Malabar spinach does some ingenious things.

■ *Left:*

In his first life, Jane Howard's monkey received calling cards in a Victorian parlor. But fitted with a parasol, he seems happier in the garden.

■ **Flowers go in and out of Jane Howard's favor with astonishing speed. This year, dahlias are good.**

As far as color is concerned, Jane Howard is iconoclastic and proud of it. She can create a riot or she can be subdued. Everything in its place. Only buff, burgundy, and venetian red are permitted on the upper terrace seen from the entry hall and dining room of her imposing house, designed by Ehrick Rossiter. Plants with burgundy accents, such as *Angelica gigas* and *Pennisetum setaceum* 'Rubrum', are welcome, but anything in blaring magenta is summarily removed ("I'd rather see dirt than the wrong color") or be-

I asked Jane Howard how she managed to carry off her particularly zany color scheme, and she divulged the formula: "I search the catalogs, looking for anything that stretches Good Taste. If the description implies that the shade verges on trashy, that's just what I want. Unless it makes me mad."

135

headed before it blossoms. Malabar spinach is acceptable, but phlox is not so fortunate. And these prejudices are forever in a state of flux. Jane Howard hates chartreuse this year, in no uncertain terms. "Didn't you adore *Ipomoea* 'Margarite' last year?" I venture. "That was last year," she chants. Flowers aren't the sole ambassadors of color. Foliage of the proper blush is equally valuable. And she really doesn't care whether a plant resides in the vegetable, fruit, or ornamental realm — beets and flowering peaches are given front-row seats.

There's a theory, and also an accompanying vocabulary, behind the madness. No sense in talking to Jane Howard if you confuse maroon with burgundy; those shades are definitely horses of vastly different colors. Although Jane Howard is new to gardening, she has rapidly garnered a reputation for calling up nurseries and inquiring what they've got available in, say, clotted blood, tawny beige, or burnt toast. She never needs plain ordinary green. Instead, she seeks "guacamole" or "turtle."

■ "If I were put under house arrest tomorrow, I'd be happy."

— *Jane Howard Hammerstein*

The feeling among Jane Howard Hammerstein's friends was that she was taking her Spirit House a tad too seriously, what with the proliferation of antique miniature Buddhas on the veranda and the incense-lighting ceremony scheduled for precisely the same time every day. So it came as no real surprise when a plastic cereal-box Bugs Bunny, baring his teeth and flexing his muscles, materialized on the scene. "I know P. Wooster did it. He knows I know. I know he knows I know." Jane Howard also knows the Spirit House will never be quite the same, is glad, and grins. Like Bugs.

*S*IMILARLY, Jane Howard is fond of affixing a name to each section of her garden, based on the personality of the place. "The Rumbles" is the water garden just below the noisy air-conditioning unit. The upper terrace of burgundy, rose, and buff is "Wine and Roses." And, as you might suspect, "Sunset Strip" is where the consummate colorist has gone berserk.

"Sunset Strip" is raucous bedlam done so defiantly that it's a masterpiece of modern art. In a nutshell, Jane Howard went for the color combination of orangeade coupled with raging pink flamingo in that particular pocket. At the center is an urn spilling with retina-splitting orange *Senecio confusus* — recently renamed *Pseudogynoxys chenopodioides*, as if botanical Latin weren't tough enough — and midnight-purple verbena topped by a raspberry-colored gazing ball of just the right proportions to save it from seeming like the cherry on a sundae. Orange tithonia, neon-hued impatiens, and purple fuchsias flock all around. It's risky business, but it's also perfectly premeditated. "If subtle peaches or

corals entered, it would just be a mess," Jane Howard confides. The area is chaos of the most carefully controlled variety. It's the Tower of Babel made to perform as a chorus.

Color is not the garden's sole venture into tongue-in-cheek. A custom-made wrought-iron fence brandishing strange curlicues, spikes, and spurs brings to mind the thorns of a rosebush. And the containers (as you might guess, of obscure shades such as metallic blue) overflow with synchronized bloom. In fact, the terraces and porches are a Pandora's box of quirkiness from every continent and era. They feature a Thai Spirit House that

looks like some sort of antique Oriental multilevel birdhouse with a population explosion of miniature Buddhas. Jane Howard lights incense on its veranda every evening. "It's a way of focusing," she says. "Resting. At first I did it for fun. Then I found it *felt* good."

THE INCENSE wafts within nostril range of an exotic life-size monkey carved of wood, with ivory choppers. Slightly menacing but also strangely droll, in his past line of work the monkey received calling cards in his outstretched hand in some High Victorian vestibule. Now he balances a parasol amid the flowers on the back porch.

The ape can be scrutinized at leisure from a nearby seating area shaded by a wisteria pergola dangling with a constellation of cacophonous tin and bronze lanterns, each one unique, all of varying vintages and such differing styles that they are in perfect disharmony.

That's just the scene immediately flanking the back door. Farther afield, other garden features enhance the property's more distant six acres. At one point, for example, a Hampton Court chimneypot stands solitarily on a magnificent rock outcropping where Jane Howard has spent long, penitential hours meticulously removing grass or encouraging moss, depending on the contours. She does it to reach enlightenment, to sharpen her focus, to finish her coffee. Another outcropping is dominated by a small, newly built octagonal room, which I was forbidden to describe. "Why?" I asked. "I don't know," Jane Howard replied. I knew. Not the right color yet. ❧

■ Not content with just any old fence, Jane Howard asked Bob Keating, a local metal artist, to design something reminiscent of a rambling rose, complete with thorns.

THE SOUND OF MUSIC

RUDYARD KIPLING HAD HIS OPINIONS about what sounds should interrupt the garden's tranquillity. As he put it in *The Glory of the Garden*, "And there you'll see the gardeners, the men and 'prentice boys / Told off to do as they are bid and do it without noise, / For except when seeds are planted and we shout to scare the birds, / The Glory of the Garden it abideth not in words."

It might well be true that the garden is no place for extraneous chatter. Still,

it isn't a particularly silent place. There's plenty of commotion going on without idle talk. It's hard enough to concentrate between the scolding of the bluejays and the drone of the katydids.

So I suppose I side with Rudyard. I see absolutely no reason to plug in a stereo speaker aimed at the great outdoors. It would break my train of thought. And a garden is the perfect place for deep introspection. One year when I planted half an acre of carrots to fill the root cellar over the winter, someone asked me what I thought about while thinning carrots. Did I write books in my head or lay plans for other gardens during my long hours on hands and knees? "No," I admitted, "I think about thinning carrots." ❧

Above: FLUTIST, AFTON VILLA, ST. FRANCISVILLE, LOUISIANA
Right: PAN, CAPRILANDS HERB FARM, COVENTRY, CONNECTICUT

Above: DIXIELAND FROGS, LES QUATRE VENTS, LA MALBAIE, QUEBEC

Let Us Give Thanks

WE WOULD LIKE TO GIVE our heartfelt thanks to the many people who helped us during the process of photographing and writing this book. In particular, we are grateful to the staff of Houghton Mifflin Company, especially for the editorial guidance of Frances Tenenbaum, Liz Duvall, and Katya Rice, and for the production skills of Jill Lazer. The book owes its whimsical design to the ingenuity of Susan McClellan. We also thank Rob Girard, Alistair Highet, and R. M. Placid Dempsey, O.S.B., for lending sympathetic ears. Words cannot express our gratitude to the gardeners who shared their wit and opened their gardens, including Mary Azarian, Michelle Billings and Carol Eaton of Downtown Ely Gardens, Bill Blass, Gretchen Bond, Frank and Anne Cabot, Caprilands Herb Farm, Amy Clarkson, Debbie Deal of Friendship Gardens, Jana Drobinsky, Beatrice Elye, Jane Howard Hammerstein, Marsha Hyll, Rachel Kane of Perennial Pleasures Nursery, Lark and Rick Levine, Nancy McCabe, Alice Moir, Peter and Su Hua Newton of Newton Vineyards, Shepherd and Ellen Ogden, Moses Pendleton, Lucinda Rooney, Kit and Marty Sagendorf, George Schoellkopf, Steve and Gail Smith of Crocker Hill Studios, the late Helen Stoddard, Morrell and Genevieve Trimble of Afton Villa, Bunny Williams, and Peter Wooster, as well as the staffs at Green Animals, Virginia House, and Vizcaya. We thank Peter Woytuk for permitting us to feature his sculpture. ❧